A Victorian School

Written by Meryl-Lynn Pluck
Illustrated by Ally Ikutani

Characters

Lovinia   **Jimmy**

Samuel   **Mr Bostock**

Miss Lavicich   **Jessie**

Miss Lavicich: And *that* is what it was like in schools during the Victorian era. Do any of you have questions? Yes, Jimmy?

Jimmy: Miss Lavicich, what kind of holograms did people watch during the Victorian era?

Miss Lavicich: There were no hologram players in the 1800s, Jimmy. Holograms are a very recent invention. Now, any more questions? Jessie?

Jessie: If holograms weren't invented how did people watch movies in the 1800s?

Miss Lavicich: Oh dear, I can see that you two don't quite get it, do you?

Jimmy: Well, it is pretty hard to imagine movies without holograms, Miss Lavicich. Maybe if we went on a field trip…

Jessie: Yes, please, Miss Lavicich. Can we use the time machine to visit a school in the Victorian era? We learned so much during our trip last month to the Middle Ages.

Jimmy and Jessie:
Please, Miss Lavicich.

Miss Lavicich: You have to promise to stay near me and behave. The rest of you carry on with your work. The three of us will be back in a **nanosecond**. And I mean it, you two. I don't want anyone getting the cane while we're there!

3

Jimmy: What's "the cane"?

Miss Lavicich: A form of punishment they used in Victorian schools. Basically, they hit pupils with a stick.

Jimmy and Jessie (*shocked*):
Don't worry! We'll behave!

Miss Lavicich: I'll just wind this dial. A date in the Victorian era… let's see… hmm, what about 1860? That ought to do it.

Jimmy: I think we're there, Miss Lavicich. Or rather, I think we're here.

Jessie: What *is* this place?

Jimmy: It looks kind of like a village. It must be a village school… though that teacher looks more like a church minister.

Mr Bostock: Silence, young man! You are not permitted to speak in my class unless you are asked. Now come in and sit down, both of you. Get your **slates** out! Come on, quickly!

Jessie (*to herself*):
Our what? (*whispering*) Jimmy, do you know what a slate is?

Jimmy: Please, sir? We don't know what a slate is.

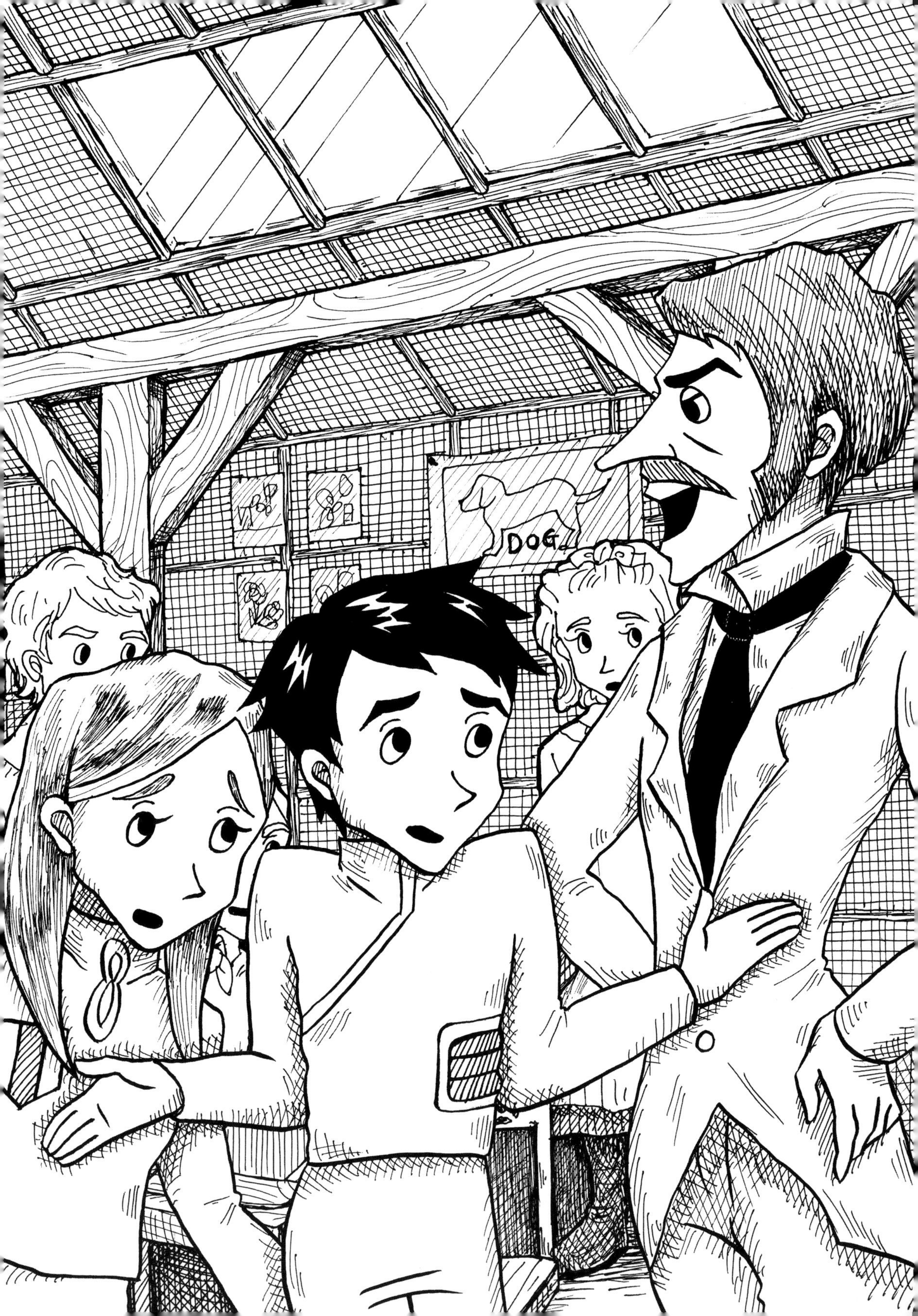
DOG

Mr Bostock: It appears you may need a little reminder then, young **dunce**. When the dinner bell goes you will take your slate to the **dunce's corner**. You will put on the **dunce's cap** and write out, "A slate is for writing on", until I tell you to stop. Now then, you lot, prepare for reading time. Quickly now!

Jimmy (*quietly*): Excuse me, I'm Jimmy and I'm new here. Could you tell me what to do, please?

Samuel (*quietly*): I thought you were new. You aren't half dressed oddly. Foreign, are you? At reading time, we meet in the south corner of the room with our reading monitor. Oh, it looks like we have a new monitor today.

Jimmy: That's Miss Lavi…

Samuel: …she must be foreign too. She's dressed as oddly as you.

Mr Bostock: Get on with it, you two!

Samuel: We all line up with our toes touching the semi-circle chalked on the floor, like this. (***more loudly***) Please, may I read first, Miss?

Miss Lavicich: Why… yes, you may. Just two sentences each please, then pass the Bible to your right, and show your neighbour where to keep reading from.

Samuel: Thank you, Miss. If you'll just show me where you'd like us to start, Miss.

Mr Bostock: Seniors, continue with your assigned tasks. Gentlemen, woodwork, and ladies, needlework. Quickly and quietly, please. And you, the new monitor, would you please keep an eye on the girls while you're listening to that reading.

Jessie (*to herself*): Needlework. No way! I'd rather do woodwork! **(*quietly*)** Excuse me, I'm new. My name's Jessie. Do you think I would be allowed to do woodwork?

Lovinia: Hello, Jessie. I'm Lovinia. There's no way you'd be allowed to do woodwork. Woodwork is for boys. We girls do needlework and housework. Why are you dressed like that?

Miss Lavicich: She's with me. We're foreigners.

Mr Bostock: Is that young woman giving you trouble? I'll soon put her to rights if she is!

Miss Lavicich: No trouble, Mr Bostock. Everything's fine.

Mr Bostock (*angrily*): Well, all right then, but just you mind. Some of these scholars are right troublemakers. But they're no match for Mr Bostock, no they aren't. If any of them give you the slightest trouble, you send them to me!

Lovinia (*quietly*): Excuse me, Miss. I meant no offence.

Miss Lavicich: None taken, but please help Jessie here. Her needlework is very rusty!

Lovinia: You haven't a clue, do you? Here, let me show you. You really must be foreign, not knowing how to do needlework and all.

Jessie: It's so cold in here. I can barely get my fingers to work. And it's so noisy! How do you ever concentrate?

Lovinia: Is it warm and quiet where you've come from, then? I wish I could visit foreign parts someday.

Jessie: Yes, and the air is a lot fresher, too.

Lovinia: The air *is* stale today, isn't it, but you soon get used to it. And at least we get to attend school in this village. In our last village, only the boys were allowed to stay on to this age.

Jessie: Why are the windows so high up?

Lovinia: To stop us looking out and being distracted from our work.

Jessie: This building isn't in very good condition, is it?

Lovinia: No, it isn't. It used to be a barn. But *all* village schools are like this. Haven't you ever been in one before? Where *do* you three come from?

Jimmy: Where's that terrible music coming from?

Samuel: It's a class outside doing **drill**.

Jimmy: Drill? What's drill?

Samuel: Drill's exercise. You know, jogging, stretching, and lifting weights in time to the music.

Jimmy: You're kidding me, right?

Samuel: No, I'm…

Mr Bostock: Time, pupils. Quickly, back to your desks. Arithmetic next, monitors. Quickly and quietly. Quickly and quietly!

Jimmy: Good, I like arithmetic. I hope it's more interesting than reading was.

Samuel: It's pretty much the same, actually. We sit in our seats, reciting and chanting like parrots. But don't you dare get anything wrong!

Lovinia: We copy and complete the sums onto our slates and then, after 15 minutes, we have to be ready to recite them by heart to Mr Bostock. And you know what he's like. Make a mistake and out comes his cane!

Jessie: Fifteen minutes!

Samuel: You're allowed to use an **abacus**… if you can find one that isn't broken.

Mr Bostock: Master Stewart, if you dare drop that abacus I'll cane you! And the same goes for you, Master Lewis, if you smudge your work! Get on with your arithmetic everyone, quickly and quietly.

Samuel (*quietly*): I've seen his new cane. He's replaced the one he broke on me last week!

Jessie: Please, Miss Lavicich, can we go back to the 21st century? I don't like it here.

Jimmy: Me neither! It's cold and noisy.

Jessie: And strict and boring…

Jimmy: …scary and smelly, too!

Jessie: And here comes Mr Bostock!

Miss Lavicich: Back to the time machine then, you two. Quick, before Mr Bostock gets here.

Jimmy and Jessie (*giggling*): Don't you mean, "Quickly and quietly!"

Lovinia: What's a time machine?

Samuel: Hey, where did they go?